10 Steps for a Young Man to Become a Great Man! : Molding a Man

Handbook

Richard J. Bias

10 Steps for a Young Man to Become a Great Man!: Molding a Man
Copyright © 2023 by Richard J. Bias

ISBN:
Paperback: 978-1959151425
e-book: 978-1959151432

The Reading Glass
BOOKS

The Reading Glass Books
1-888-420-3050
www.readingglassbooks.com
production@readingglassbooks.com

Contents

Preview

This handbook has been created to provide some good information and knowledge for young men. The information hopefully will start each young man off on their journey through life on the right track. This book will cover, and review information also add things that need to be discuss. No one knows everything and having a handy dandy book that young men can read through to reinforce they decision is a plus. There will be times when young men may feel unsure of what their about do. This would be one of those times when having a copy of my book has value. I strongly suggest that each young men get one or is given a copy of this book to help them navigate life. Life is too short for regrets and having a copy of this book may be an invaluable asset for any young men 13 to 25 years old.

Not often is there a chance to read something that can have a profound impact on life as the one this book will provide. What this book offers is a variety of information that is not readily available in this form. The information in the book is design and categorized to lead the reader through a developing process. The developing process will allow the reader to perform or accomplish each level items. There is no set-in stone way of accomplishing each item, but it would make the process smoother. Having an orderly process can always make life a little easier. For the young men that are starting their life journey would do well to follow the books process. There are any number of "If I had only" statements made by young men after the fact.

The reason why I decided to write this book was because there is nothing out today that lays out this information this way. The information cover things that all young men will need to know or do at some time in their life. The advantage of having all these important requirements all in one book is priceless. Depending on the young man age some of the required items will be out of reach. Having an advanced knowledge of things to come will ensure that the young man is prepared. There is a lot to be said for the man who is prepared and ready for life's requirements. Many things can get overlooked, forgotten that can cause delays. But having a copy of this book will place valuable information at your fingertips.

1. <u>Know You're Here for Something Great!</u>

There is one question that everyone asks themselves. What am I here for? Why was I put on earth? There are traditional concepts for why people were put on earth. These concepts breakdown the roles between "Men & Women." Through the years these concepts have been under discussion as to the real relevance today. Young men have a unique physical ability that allows them to accomplish harder task. This ability has defined some specific functions and areas that men are better at preforming. Not every man is able to succeed at all function but there is something for everyone. Finding what they are good at, or they love doing is the ultimate plan.

Allowing yourself time to develop and grow into your mature mental and physical being is a must. Exploring any and all of your mental and physical abilities helps you focus on the one skill you do best. Once this skill is identified you can now prepare to train and develop it to perfection. If you discover that you have a few skills that you're good at, then practice with all of them. Training each one with the amount of enthusiasm to how much you enjoy doing the skill. Don't put to much effort into skills that are not the best skill or one you've priories less than another.

Who is this person that inside your body? Every young person goes through this growth period. It normal to be curious about who you are and why you're here. This is the quest that everyone has been tasked with defining who you are. We go through life day after day trying to discover this identity. What purpose were we put on earth to accomplish? It's up to each person to discover and define their reason for being on earth. No one can tell you your reason for being on earth. It's a journey that will require you to search and discover that elusive path.

Everyone is given their own passion, vision, and purpose that must be pursued.

Passion = strong and powerful emotion

Vision = an idea or mental image of something.

Purpose = intention to achieve a positive mark on the world.

It is each person's responsibility to figure out what each one of those three traits may be. This is an individual process that only you can complete. No one else can know what you are here on earth to accomplish. Everyone can provide something useful to this world. People just have to be willing to put in the work to search for their own truth. It's a challenge for young men to search for something unknown but that is where the fun comes from. No one said life would be easy but living life with a purpose is key.

One of life's mystery is that some people distinguish themselves intellectually. They have been given the gift of intellectual competence. Which allow them to focus their mind on a specific way not everyone can do. Having this intellectual ability will define what type of skills they should pursue. This set them apart from other people and provide a different path to travel. This path will take nothing different to accomplish a valuable outcome. The energy and effort needed will have the same requirements in the end. This skill will provide the world with much needed information and data that can add life sustaining things.

Intellect = brilliant mind; power of knowing; reasoning & understanding

Another of life's mystery is that some people are born with a physical ability that surpasses many people. This physical ability also must be developed and cultivated. No one can control how their physical ability will turn out unless they put in the work with the discipline to finish. Depending on the specific skill and training designed to enhance the physical ability means everything. The individual focus of the young man is the key component. How much you want your specific gift to grow is a personal thing.

Physical ability = Stamina; strength; velocity, speed, and agility

As you process through all these particular aspects of your life understanding that everyone has the same ordeal to complete. No one is exempted from figuring out what greatness they are here to deliver. People are given the ability to choose their own path in life. This is where each person's individual preference can be one of the most important points of life success. Sometimes in life, without proper guidance or understanding of the world's dynamics you can get lost. This information is designed to provide some information insight into what you can do to prepare yourself to succeed.

2. <u>Concentrate on your Special Skills.</u>

Once you have discovered exactly what special skills that you've been blessed with focus on that skill. Many people want to have curtain skill and they try hard to perfect their ability but fall short. Not everyone can become a superstar in their life but that's no reason to not try. Sometime a low skill can be turned into a high-level skill with determination. It's all about how much the person want to be good at that skill. If you put in the work nothing can stop you from reaching what you desire. The only person who can stop you is you! Being able to control your mindset to pursue the desired goal is a special skill in itself.

There are many specific requirements that must be met in order to develop your skill to perfection. These requirements cannot be taken lightly if you want great results. Lots of people think that there is a short cut to accomplish anything. They are all the one's that come in second and not first. There are no short cuts to becoming great. Everyone must do the required work to achieve a great outcome. Don't think or let anyone tell you that it can be done tomorrow. That would possibly be one of the reasons you don't reach your goal. How your life turns out is up to you no one else.

The amount of effort that each person applies to completing or accomplishing their desired goal shows how much they want to achieve that end. Everyone has the ability to or right to give whatever amount of effort that they want. But that level of effort will determine how well your special ability will improve. The more the effort the better, less effort will produce lower skilled ability. Everyone has control of their destiny and what kind of life they will live.

Effort = "Physical or mental activity needed to achieve something, vigorous or determined attempt"

One of the pivotal reasons why some people reach a high level of their special skill is because of focus. Some people understand that implementing the proper degree of focus can ensure their desired result will be obtained. Knowing that there needs to be a specific amount of concentration on that special skill is key for any improvement. This mindset will surely lead to a successful development of improving that special skill. The desired outcome of improving those skills is the dream.

Focus = concentrate attention and effort, Clear vision, center of interest or activity.

An important requirement that can ensure the greatest level of development is to refine your process. As you work through the routine of developing the skill there will be areas that can be adjusted. Some changes may require less time and others may improve efficiency. The benefit of taking the time to review the process can bring about unforeseen rewards. Nothing is set in stone as the "end all be all" process for success. Everything can benefit from having a second look to review the process.

> Refine = "Improve something, remove impurities or unwanted elements, making small changes"

Nothing can stop a young man from accomplishing his goal if his "will power" is strong. Determination can be the main element of how rewarding and successful the journey ends. Let no one tell you that its going to be easy and you don't have to put all your time into the skill. Human nature has proven that some people can sabotage your dream to gain an advantage. That's just a part of life that not everyone has your best interests in their plan. We must always have an unshakeable belief in ourselves and the journey that we are on.

3. <u>Develop your Personal Manly Habits.</u>

Man has advanced to a level of human awareness that allow us to care for our wellbeing naturally. The body has very specific needs to ensure that it remains disease free. Everyone is expected to do daily personal health care every day. This standard is adhered to on an individual level. It has become a mark of separation for each person to be judge. There are some people who will fall short of this standard and be consider different. Each man must take their own position on personal health care. But must understand that some decisions come with consequences.

Hygiene = "Practice or activity that you do to keep yourself healthy and clean"

Bathing: is one of the basic practices that everyone is supposed to do. It can be done in the tub or shower and is the act of cleaning the whole body with soap and water. Living in a civilized society is a privilege that people on earth enjoy. Everyone is free to live within this world as they see fit. The problem comes when some people done want to perform the basic task of bathing. This problem can create a big problem that causes a pandemic.

Mouth care: is accomplished by brushing your teeth using a toothbrush and toothpaste. This action must be continued for two minutes and done in a circular motion. The required method is to brush after every meal equals three times a day. Another part of mouth care is keeping your breath fresh. It's done by using mouthwash after brushing your teeth and also brushing the tongue. Having a dental check-up twice a year is a recommendation for Mouth Care.

Hair care: is a very visible part of everyone's personal appearance that can have a negative or positive look. The proper way of caring for your hair is to wash it and then apply hair care ointment. Combing or brushing will create a very special look. It's a traditional type of hair care to get a haircut at the barber shop. Men discuss a lot of meaningful things at the barber shop.

Shaving: is one of the oldest actions performed by men and needs to be learned to do it right. Preparing you face is required for the best outcome. Using warm water or warm towel before applying the shaving cream. The razer must be position so it goes in the right direction. Don't go against the grain of how the hair grows. It will cause the hair to grow under the skin (ingrown) if the hair is cut the wrong way.

Hand and foot care: these are some of the most neglected areas on the body. Cutting your fingernails is a sure sign of a person's maturity and is easily viewed. The toenails are another area that displays your level of hygiene. So, cutting the toenails are just as important to your health. The feet require some specific care to combat foot odor and athlete's foot. There are some ointments that can help keep your feet healthy.

Body lotion: is one of the most misunderstood aspects of your personal hygiene that can cause adverse effects. Applying specific kinds of facial cream are necessary for facial skin health. Using the proper type of body lotion can improve the bodies overall look and it feel better. Appling lotion on a daily basis will reduce the possibility of skin irritation. The body can have some very unpleasant feelings of itching and lotion helps.

Knowing and using personal manly habits is a practice that will provide you the confidence of self-awareness. There are not many things that can improve how you value yourself more than personal hygiene. It's such a simple part of life but can have a profound effect on your life. There are many different outcomes that can be realized as a result of how well you take care of yourself. Personal hygiene may seem like a small trivial task, but it can have a huge result on how the world reacts to you as a man.

4. <u>Learn your Own Interpersonal Skills.</u>

We all sooner or later will come into contact with that important someone each and every day for the rest of your life. How well you are able to interact with that person will affect the possible future outcomes with that person. Having an ability to communicate with people is important for creating friendships and professional relationships. There are lots of advantages that can be gain from having a good professional relationship. Which can possibly increase the future possibilities of monitory gain. Improving some specific skills and traits that are key to how well you communicate is critical.

Language & Speech is a key component to how well you can express your opinion. Developing a large vocabulary and practicing your individual speech pronunciation is very important. Practicing in front of a mirror or in front of a family member can be a game changer. Everyone you meet will be judging you in the next few moments to decide whether they want to continue the conversation. Preparing yourself to display the best you will determine a lot of your future success. Everyone want to be successful so put in the work and become that one.

Handshake: can have a first impression that offers highly regarded one on one acknowledgment. There is only one proper way to initiate and preform a handshake. The process needs to be done with a firm gripe that shows confidence. The traditional time to hold a handshake is two to three seconds. The handshake is one skill that must be mastered to ensure a good reception in all your interactions. Properly preform it will leave a great first impression on that person you met. It said that "first impression" are priceless in the professional world.

Eye contact: One of the most important and obvious skill that tents to be misunderstood and misused is eye contact. There is a critical component of communication that eye contact provides. The most excepted way to use eye contact is holding it for four to five seconds. There is an unspoken advantage to using eye contact during communication with people. This skill must not be overlooked as an important aspect of communication. We all need to have every advantage available to be a success eye contact is definitely one.

Eye Contact defined: "maintain appropriate eye contact without staring, you should maintain eye contact for 50 percent of the time while speaking and 70% of the time while listening."

It's natural for people to interact with each other and communicate their wants or needs. This is an acceptable norm to communication with each other that society has created. We are able to develop commerce which allow everyone to make a living. Through communicating we learn what each of us may have to offer that might be useful in our daily life.

Not being able to communicate would make it harder for everyone to survive. Human purification is depended on how well we can understand each other.

It is the responsibility of everyone to communicate and do it effectively to ensure that we understand each other. If we don't understand or misunderstand what someone is trying to tell us. There can be problem that cause undue harm or bad result that take our livelihood away. The most important aspect of human interaction is communication. Take the time to improve your ability to communicate on a personal level.

5. <u>Cultivate your Personal Fashion Style.</u>

Every man is judged on how well dressed or how update his fashion style is refined. Knowing fashion and style is another growing area that society is requiring men to be aware of now. It no longer a brainless action of just putting on any you want without proper coordination. There now must be attention paid to what color goes with each item. This personal preference area of fashion is a positive or negative depending on the trend at the time. Learning the ins and outs of fashion can be a game changer with relationships. This can include both personal and professional relationships.

Wardrobe: All men must have a collection of clothes that spans each season of the year. There must be a color standard that can be versatile and used across the spectrum. It must fall within the limits of a normal men's wardrobe requirements. There are very specific clothing items that men are required to have in their personal wardrobe. As we travel through our journey in life some specific moments and events will arise that we must attended. Having the proper attire for that event is a sign of maturity. That's what every man wants, to be considered a mature man.

Every man should have a wardrobe that consist of the proper clothing items for each season. There must be a set of Winter items that provide cold weather protection. The protection needs to be properly worn with three layers deep for the best result.

The Spring items will provide semi weather protection for the temperature changes that take place. These items can be of a colorful variety that adds style to the collection. There is a delicate balance that color play in stating your fashion style preference. Some global locations can provide a color palette that allows brighter designs as normal ware.

The Summer clothes items can be of a lighter and cooler fabric and material. Summer items mainly consist of shorts, t-shirts, bathing suits and flip flops. This is an acceptable and normal wardrobe design that should be part of every man's dress code.

The fall clothing items can now start to increase with the thickness of the fabric. The fall weather change will dictate how warm the clothing needs to be based on the temperature change. The wardrobe must include two suits black and blue colors and dress shoes. These items are needed for any of the formal events we all must attend. These normal items added to the wardrobe will be prove of maturity for the young man. Here are some wardrobe suggestions to start the journey.

A Traditional and Normal Wardrobe Consists of the Following Items:

Suit Dark

Sport Coat

Over Coat

Light-Dark Dress Shirt

Ties

Dress Shoes

Short Sleeved Polo

T-Shirts

Shorts

Underwear

Socks

Bathing Suit

Dress- Casual Slacks

Blue Jeans

Casual Footwear

Work Boots

Sandals-Flip Flops

Hat

Wardrobe Accessories for Men:

Casual Watch
Dress Watch X
Ring
Bracelet
Sunglasses
Pen
Tie bar
Cufflinks
Scarf

6. <u>Research your Own Personal Identity Presents.</u>

Every person on earth needs to have personal identification that certify who they are for legal purposes. Identification is an essential item that must be requested to receive the certification. There is no place that people go which won't require some type of ID. ID allows people to pursue their dreams of employment or hopes of business ownership. Having an identity present will make life much easier to move throughout the world. There are some specific types of paperwork that must be created for each person.

Birth certificate: is the first one piece of identification that everyone gets. It must be produced by the medical facility that the person was born in. There must be a certified copy of the form created and used in order to get any of the other types of ID required. The copy should be kept in a safe place to protect the form. A new copy can be requested through the state of origin if needed.

Social Security Card: is the second piece of ID that people will receive once they want to enter the employment market. Having a social security number will allows a person to get employed. It can also be used as a form of ID that is sometimes requested as prove of your existence. The card is important by knowing your SSN number will be good enough.

Driver License: this is one of the most popular forms of ID that everyone can get. The privilege of driving is rewarded after passing the test. It's just as easy to take away the privilege if it is abused. Every young man dreams of one day driving a car. But must learn the responsibilities that comes along with that privilege. It has a small drawback that it must be renew every year.

Individual ID: there is a federal or state level ID that can be requested and granted. This is just an additional form of ID that available to everyone. It not an necessity to have it just an additional form of ID that makes life easier. Sometime there are situations that require three forms of ID to do business with curtain organizations. So having three forms of ID in a personal plus.

Passport: is a federal form of ID that can take the place of all the other form of ID except a driver license. But it is valid throughout the world as prove of ID as to who you are. A passport come with a lot of social status for those who have one. It not easily received if your background has problem, and they will search your past.

7. <u>Think About your Mobility Option.</u>

There are some important mobile and technology devices that makes life easier to move throughout the world. The fast-paced level of society has made it almost impossible to function without having some form of technology. Having the ability to get from place to place is a necessity. People cannot travel form place to place without having some form of technology. Being able to contact or staying in touch with people and family member is a very important security option. So having some or one type of mobile technology devices can be a stress reliever.

Mobile Phone: is the latest item of technology that has transform the way we communicate. It allows us to stay in touch over long distances and perform some work-related tasks while you out of the office. The technology is a convenience that can give you a false sense of security. It must be used with caution and treated as just an added piece of luxury. Mobile phone can come with many security measures. But using those security features properly make all the difference. We can store a lot of personal information that we don't want open to the public. These technology devices must be treated with precaution on a daily basis.

Automobile: one of the most highly used and visible form of technology advancement is the car. Having a car makes your ability get from place to place an easier task. Driving a car is one of the most coveted desires felt by everyone in the modern world. The responsibility of owning a car is a privilege that everyone can be given. It can also be taken away if the privilege is abused. It must be operated and used within the rules of the road. No one can drive or operate a car without the proper paperwork. The documentation to drive a car consist of vehicle registration, auto insurance and personal driver's license.

Laptop computer: this technology has changed the way we think about work and going into the office. Laptops having wireless capability and using the internet allows people to work from home. This wireless internet access has provided the world with a new way to communicate. Utilizing a laptop and wireless technology today is a game changer. It allows people to reach and pursue new and different areas of opportunity. The Wi-Fi age has open up this world environment to everyone willing to discover the use and needs in that universe.

8. <u>Consider your Higher Education Option.</u>

This world is continuing to evolve with technology advancement that don't seem to be slowing down. There will be a highly advanced job environment that needs to have people who can work within it. These job positions will require individuals that are educated in that field of study. All the young men need to think about and prepare for this eventuality. The only option that can provide the needed solution is education. If getting a higher education is not in your future, then these high paying salary position will pass you by.

Degree: the most important form of education is getting a four-year degree. Most employer's will consider having a degree as prove of your intellect. They view having a degree as prove that you can finish the task. It can be view that you honor your commitments. These are all good traits that employer look for in job applicates. Having some secondary education in technology course will add a possible plus to your resume. Education will always be an advantage to any eligible job seeking person.

Certification: are another form of education that can provide an advantage in specific field of employment. There are a range of certifications available that can provide a variety of option to pursue that can narrow the path. There's many of the union trade job skills that come with certs, Carpenter, electrician, plumber also HVAC Tech. Some of the highly technical job skill that have certs are the computer technology fields, Network, Security, Server, Desktop support. The job opportunities today are at every young man's fingertip if only they take the chance.

Sponsorship programs: there are specific employment opportunities that provide quick start positions. These positions require a curtain amount of commitment to get the opportunity. But a lot of the earlier mention field come with that type of opportunity if you're willing to commit to the company. There will probably be some type of written agreement that must be signed. The contract might have some very strict requirements so pursue only those position that you will enjoy doing.

There are no guarantees in this world that everyone will succeed but that no reason not to try. Prepare yourself by leaving no doubt that your commit to yourself to follow through will this plan. Figure out what your purpose is and plan to achieve that goal. Nothing will happen until you make the first move by taking that large step to start.

9. <u>Discuss your Financial Status.</u>

Everything in this world that people want will cost some amount of money. Everyone will need money to survive and live day to day. It goes without saying that money makes the world go round. Earning any amount of money will require having a skill to do a job. Employment is a critical part of daily life for most people in the world. There's no way around needing money to survive. Money can be what helps you be happy, or it can make you miserable. So, know about financial status and working to build your own financial freedom is good.

Having financial intelligence is an important part of successfully surviving in this world. Preparing for the accumulation of money needs is the first step in securing your future. Most people do it through employment and a saving plan that will increase in value. There are a lot of different financial entities that provide some specific type of saving options. A financial planner is a good choice when looking to plan with your money for the future. Setting up a safe place the put your money is a very important decision.

Bank account: A bank is the most commonly used institution to put the money you earn in for safe keeping.

Bank will require proper identification to open an account in their institution. Most companies require that you have a bank account for direct deposit. Because it's the easiest way to pay employee by using direct deposit and it takes less paper. Having a checking account and a saving account will be a smart decision for saving money. These two accounts can provide another way to save money for the future.

Credit card: debt is a double edge sword that can be a plus when people look at your worth. Having too much debt can cause all kind of hardship on people. Large amounts of debt can have a negative effect on possible future transaction that require a good ratio between debt and income. So having credit is great but not if it consumed by debt. There is a fine line that everyone must walk down to pursue their financial freedom. It one of life's pleasure.

IRA, 401K, Roth: these are saving options that need to be discuss with professional financial people to ensure you get it right. These saving entities do have some great advantages to reaching your saving goal quicker. But somethings are better left to the professional and ones you can trust. Nothing get done without a cost so be warmed.

10. <u>Plan your Next 5-to-10-year Goals.</u>

It's important for everyone to know where your headed and where you will end up in life. This awareness will provide a clear understanding and path that can enable you to succeed. There are many options that can define your future goals. But as long as you have a written design plan to your future goals, it is possible to envision them being accomplishing. This tool can provide motivation that keeps you on track and stay dedicated to your dream.

One of the most commonly used plans is a "Five to Ten" year goal plan. It is designed to have milestones that track the progress through meeting each smaller goal. If you look back through these ten steps and actually map them into your 5-to-10-year goal plan it's a start. Each of those items will become good milestone marker to keep you on track to reach your final goal. It's a simple process if you take the time to start. There are plenty of planner in different design to satisfy everyone.

Below is an example of a 5-year plan:

Goals	Year1	Year2	Year3	Year4	Year5
Professional	certs	cert#2	MBA		
Career	junior PM	PM	Senior PM	Regional PM	
Financial	Savings	Saving	Saving	Buy a home.	
Health	Diet exer.	do 5k	half mara.		Full marathon
Travel		Asia		Europe	

There is nothing more rewarding than accomplishing your goals. Even completing small goal give you some measure of accomplishment. Having a plan is the beginning of something great and you will accomplish that greatness. Put the plan into effect and start your journey through life. The only thing holding you back is you start your story today. Let yourself have a dream for the future and make it come to life.

Don't worry about how professional the plan may look just put the information down. Once the information is on the paper, you'll be able to go back and revive and correct where it's needed. Anything can be changed as long as there's time to execute it and time to complete it. Doing something for your future will indirectly effect everyone around you. That's put the world on notice!

Closure

I would like to thank you for choosing my handbook that I hope is helpful. There is a need in this world to develop young men that can make a difference. It must start somewhere, and I chose bringing the transformation through the young men around the world. The future of this planet will one day rest on the shoulder of the younger generation. I want to prepare this younger generation to take up the responsibility with pride and carry-on a civil living environment.

There must be a civil living environment so the world can continue to exist. If we allow this toxic chao to continue around the world were doomed. I've had the opportunity to travel around the world to different country. I found that the people in these other countries don't hate other races. They're just trying to live like everyone else and go to work to pay their bills. The only hatred that exists is what's being taught to them by certain people and governments.

My dream is to see a world where all the people on the earth can live in harmony. This is a concept that some people will call a "pipe dream" and say it can never happen. But if everyone that had a dream listened to the nah sayer none of the technology advancements we use today would be available. So, I will believe in my faith and let our higher power decided the outcome. Thank You!

www.ingramcontent.com/pod-product-compliance
Lightning Source LLC
Chambersburg PA
CBHW032104020426
42335CB00011B/485